Crisco

DELICIOUS
Desserts for All Occasions

CHERRY CHEESE BARS

BASE
     1 cup walnut pieces, divided
1 1/4 cups all-purpose flour
     1/2 cup firmly packed light
          brown sugar
     1/2 Butter Flavor CRISCO® Stick
          or 1/2 cup Butter Flavor
          CRISCO® all-vegetable
          shortening plus additional
          for greasing
     1/2 cup flake coconut

FILLING
     2 packages (8 ounces each)
          cream cheese, softened
     2/3 cup granulated sugar
     2 eggs
     2 teaspoons vanilla
     1 can (21 ounces) cherry pie
          filling*

*You may substitute another fruit pie filling
for the cherry pie filling.*

1. Heat oven to 350°F. Grease
13×9×2-inch pan with shortening.
Place cooling rack on countertop.

2. Chop 1/2 cup nuts coarsely.
Reserve for topping. Chop remaining
1/2 cup nuts finely.

3. For base, combine flour and
brown sugar in medium bowl. Cut in
1/2 cup shortening until fine crumbs
form. Add 1/2 cup finely chopped
nuts and coconut. Mix well. Reserve
1/2 cup crumbs for topping. Press
remaining crumbs in bottom of pan.
Bake at 350°F for 12 to 15 minutes
or until edges are lightly browned.
Do not overbake.

4. For filling, combine cream
cheese, granulated sugar, eggs and
vanilla in small bowl. Beat at
medium speed of electric mixer until
well blended. Spread over hot baked
base. Return to oven. Bake for
15 minutes. *Do not overbake.*

5. Spread cherry pie filling over
cheese layer.

6. Combine reserved coarsely
chopped nuts and reserved crumbs.
Sprinkle over pie filling. Return to
oven. Bake for 15 minutes. *Do not
overbake.* Cool in pan on cooling
rack. Refrigerate several hours. Cut
into 2×1 1/2-inch bars.
Makes 3 dozen bars

Kitchen Hint. . . . . . .

**Store brown sugar in a sealed
plastic bag. It stays moist,
measures easily and can be
packed into a cup through the
bag—no more sticky hands.**

Cherry Cheese Bars

SUN DRIED CRANBERRY–WALNUT OATMEAL COOKIES

3/4 Butter Flavor CRISCO® Stick
   or 3/4 cup Butter Flavor
   CRISCO® all-vegetable
   shortening
3/4 cup granulated sugar
3/4 cup firmly packed light
   brown sugar
 2 eggs
 1 teaspoon vanilla
 1 cup all-purpose flour
 1 teaspoon baking soda
1/4 teaspoon salt
23/4 cups rolled oats
 1 cup sun dried cranberries
 1 cup walnut pieces

1. Heat oven to 375°F.

2. Combine 3/4 cup shortening and sugars in large bowl. Beat at medium speed with electric mixer until well blended. Beat in eggs and vanilla until well blended.

3. Combine flour, baking soda and salt in small bowl. Stir into creamed mixture; mix well. Add oats, sun dried cranberries and walnuts. Spray cookie sheets with CRISCO® No-Stick Cooking Spray. Dust with flour. Drop dough by teaspoonfuls about 2 inches apart onto prepared cookie sheets. Bake at 375°F for 8 minutes or until firm and brown. Cool on cookie sheets 4 minutes; transfer to cooling rack.

Makes about 6 dozen cookies

CHEF'S "MIDNIGHT SNACK" CHOCOLATE CHIP COOKIES

 1 CRISCO® Stick or 1 cup
   CRISCO® all-vegetable
   shortening
 1 cup granulated sugar
1/2 cup firmly packed light
   brown sugar
 2 eggs
 2 teaspoons vanilla
1/2 teaspoon baking powder
1/4 teaspoon salt
21/4 cups cake flour
 1 pound chocolate chips

1. Combine 1 cup shortening and sugars in large bowl. Beat on medium speed with electric mixer until well blended. Beat in eggs, vanilla, baking powder and salt until well blended. Stir in cake flour.

2. Stir in chocolate chips just until mixed in. Shape dough into two rolls about 2 inches in diameter. Wrap tightly in plastic and refrigerate 4 hours or overnight.

3. Heat oven to 350°F.

4. Slice dough about 1/2 inch thick. Place slices on ungreased cookie sheets. Bake at 350°F for 10 to 14 minutes or until firm and golden. Cool on cookie sheets 4 minutes; transfer to cooling racks.

Makes about 4 dozen cookies

*Sun Dried Cranberry–
Walnut Oatmeal Cookies*

Crisco.com We cook.

FROSTED HOLIDAY CUT–OUTS

1¼ cups granulated sugar
1 Butter Flavor CRISCO® Stick or 1 cup Butter Flavor CRISCO® all-vegetable shortening
2 eggs
¼ cup light corn syrup or regular pancake syrup
1 tablespoon vanilla
3 cups plus 4 tablespoons all-purpose flour, divided
¾ teaspoon baking powder
½ teaspoon baking soda
½ teaspoon salt

ICING
1 cup confectioners' sugar
2 tablespoons milk
Food color (optional)
Decorating icing

1. Combine sugar and 1 cup shortening in large bowl. Beat at medium speed of electric mixer until well blended. Add eggs, syrup and vanilla; beat until well blended and fluffy. Combine 3 cups flour, baking powder, baking soda and salt in medium bowl. Gradually add to shortening mixture, beating at low speed until well blended. Divide dough into 4 equal pieces; shape each into disk. Wrap with plastic wrap. Refrigerate 1 hour or until firm.

2. Heat oven to 375°F. Place sheets of foil on countertop for cooling cookies. Sprinkle about 1 tablespoon flour on large sheet of waxed paper. Place disk of dough on floured paper; flatten slightly with hands. Turn dough over; cover with another large sheet of waxed paper. Roll dough to ¼-inch thickness. Remove top sheet of waxed paper. Cut into desired shapes with floured cookie cutters. Place 2 inches apart on ungreased baking sheet. Repeat with remaining dough.

3. Bake one baking sheet at a time at 375°F for 5 to 7 minutes or until edges of cookies are lightly browned. *Do not overbake.* Cool 2 minutes on baking sheet. Remove cookies to foil to cool completely.

4. For icing, combine confectioners' sugar and milk; stir until smooth. Add food color, if desired. Stir until blended. Spread icing on cookies; place on foil until icing is set. Decorate as desired with decorating icing.
Makes about 3½ dozen cookies

Kitchen Hint. . . . . . .

Before you begin frosting and decorating the cookies, place waxed paper under the wire rack to keep your counters clean and make cleanup easier.

 Crisco.com **We cook.**

HAYSTACKS

¼ Butter Flavor CRISCO® Stick
   or ¼ cup Butter Flavor
   CRISCO® all-vegetable
   shortening
½ cup JIF® Creamy Peanut
   Butter
2 cups butterscotch-flavored
   chips
6 cups corn flakes
⅔ cup semisweet miniature
   chocolate chips
   Chopped peanuts or
   chocolate jimmies
   (optional)

1. Combine ¼ cup shortening, peanut butter and butterscotch chips in large microwave-safe bowl. Cover with waxed paper. Microwave at 50% (MEDIUM). Stir after 1 minute. Repeat until smooth (or melt on rangetop in small saucepan on very low heat, stirring constantly).

2. Pour corn flakes into large bowl. Pour hot butterscotch mixture over flakes. Stir with spoon until flakes are coated. Stir in chocolate chips.

3. Spoon scant ¼ cup mixture into mounds on waxed paper-lined baking sheets. Sprinkle with chopped nuts, if desired. Refrigerate until firm.
Makes about 3 dozen cookies

P.B. GRAHAM SNACKERS

½ Butter Flavor CRISCO® Stick
   or ½ cup Butter Flavor
   CRISCO® all-vegetable
   shortening
2 cups confectioners' sugar
¾ cup JIF® Creamy Peanut
   Butter
1 cup graham cracker crumbs
½ cup semisweet chocolate
   chips
½ cup graham cracker crumbs
   or crushed peanuts or
   colored sugar or sprinkles
   (optional)

1. Combine ½ cup shortening, confectioners' sugar and peanut butter in large bowl. Beat at low speed with electric mixer until well blended. Stir in 1 cup crumbs and chocolate chips. Cover and refrigerate 1 hour.

2. Form dough into 1-inch balls. Roll in ½ cup crumbs, peanuts, colored sugar or sprinkles. Cover and refrigerate until ready to serve.
Makes about 3 dozen cookies

COCONUT POUND CAKE

CAKE

- 2 cups granulated sugar
- 1 Butter Flavor CRISCO® Stick or 1 cup Butter Flavor CRISCO® all-vegetable shortening plus additional for greasing
- 5 eggs
- 1 1/2 teaspoons coconut extract
- 2 1/4 cups all-purpose flour
- 1 1/2 teaspoons baking powder
- 1/2 teaspoon salt
- 1 cup buttermilk or sour milk*
- 1 cup shredded coconut, chopped

GLAZE

- 1/2 cup granulated sugar
- 1/4 cup water
- 1 1/2 teaspoons coconut extract

GARNISH (OPTIONAL)

- Whipped topping or whipped cream
- Assorted fresh fruit

*To sour milk: Combine 1 tablespoon white vinegar plus enough milk to equal 1 cup. Stir. Wait 5 minutes before using.

1. Heat oven to 350°F. Grease 10-inch tube pan with shortening. Flour lightly. Place cooling rack on countertop to cool cake.

2. For cake, combine 2 cups sugar and 1 cup shortening in large bowl. Beat at medium speed of electric mixer until blended. Add eggs, 1 at a time, beating slightly after each addition. Beat in 1 1/2 teaspoons coconut extract.

3. Combine flour, baking powder and salt in medium bowl. Add alternately with buttermilk to creamed mixture, beating at low speed after each addition until well blended. Add coconut. Mix until blended. Spoon into pan.

4. Bake at 350°F for 50 minutes or until toothpick inserted in center comes out clean. *Do not overbake.* Remove to wire rack. Cool for 5 minutes. Remove cake from pan. Place cake, top side up, on serving plate. Use toothpick to poke 12 to 15 holes in top of cake.

5. For glaze, combine 1/2 cup sugar, water and 1 1/2 teaspoons coconut extract in small saucepan. Cook and stir over medium heat until mixture comes to a boil. Remove from heat. Cool 15 minutes. Spoon over cake. Cool completely.

6. For optional garnish, place spoonfuls of whipped topping and assorted fresh fruit on each serving.

Makes one 10-inch tube cake (12 to 16 servings)

Coconut Pound Cake

CINNAMON ROLL COOKIES

CINNAMON MIXTURE
   ¼ cup granulated sugar
   **1 tablespoon ground
      cinnamon**

COOKIE DOUGH
   **1 Butter Flavor CRISCO® Stick
      or 1 cup Butter Flavor
      CRISCO® all-vegetable
      shortening**
   **1 cup firmly packed light
      brown sugar**
   2 eggs
   1 teaspoon vanilla
   3 cups all-purpose flour
   2 teaspoons baking powder
   ½ teaspoon salt
   1 teaspoon ground cinnamon

1. For cinnamon mixture, combine granulated sugar and 1 tablespoon cinnamon in small bowl; mix well. Set aside.

2. For cookie dough, combine 1 cup shortening and brown sugar in large bowl. Beat at medium speed with electric mixer until well blended. Beat in eggs and vanilla until well blended.

3. Combine flour, baking powder, salt and 1 teaspoon cinnamon in small bowl. Add to creamed mixture; mix well.

4. Turn dough onto sheet of waxed paper. Spread dough into 9×6-inch rectangle using rubber spatula. Sprinkle with 4 tablespoons cinnamon mixture to within 1 inch from edge. Roll up jelly-roll style into log. Dust log with remaining cinnamon mixture. Wrap tightly in plastic wrap; refrigerate 4 hours or overnight.

5. Heat oven to 350°F. Spray cookie sheets with CRISCO® No-Stick Cooking Spray.

6. Slice dough ¼ inch thick. Place on prepared cookie sheets. Bake at 350°F for 8 minutes or until lightly browned on top. Cool on cookie sheets 4 minutes; transfer to cooling racks.

Makes about 5 dozen cookies

Kitchen Hint. . . . . . .

Be careful when working with this dough. Since it is a stiff dough, it can crack easily when it is rolled. Roll the dough slowly and smooth any cracks with your finger as you go.

Cinnamon Roll Cookies

ST. PAT'S PINWHEELS

1 1/4 cups granulated sugar
1 Butter Flavor CRISCO® Stick
  or 1 cup Butter Flavor
  CRISCO® all-vegetable
  shortening
2 eggs
1/4 cup light corn syrup or
  regular pancake syrup
1 tablespoon vanilla
3 cups all-purpose flour plus
  2 tablespoons, divided
3/4 teaspoon baking powder
1/2 teaspoon baking soda
1/2 teaspoon salt
1/2 teaspoon peppermint
  extract
Green food color

1. Place sugar and 1 cup shortening in large bowl. Beat at medium speed of electric mixer until well blended. Add eggs, syrup and vanilla; beat until well blended and fluffy.

2. Combine 3 cups flour, baking powder, baking soda and salt. Add gradually to shortening mixture, beating at low speed until well blended.

3. Place half of dough in medium bowl. Stir in peppermint extract and food color, a few drops at a time, until desired shade of green. Shape each dough into disk. Wrap with plastic wrap. Refrigerate several hours or until firm.

4. Sprinkle about 1 tablespoon flour on large sheet of waxed paper. Place peppermint dough on floured paper; flatten slightly with hands. Turn dough over; cover with another large sheet of waxed paper. Roll dough into 14×9-inch rectangle. Set aside. Repeat with plain dough.

5. Remove top sheet of waxed paper from both doughs. Invert plain dough onto peppermint dough, aligning edges carefully. Remove waxed paper from plain dough. Trim dough to form rectangle. Roll dough tightly in jelly-roll fashion starting with long side and using bottom sheet of waxed paper as guide, removing waxed paper during rolling. Wrap roll in waxed paper; freeze at least 30 minutes or until very firm.

6. Heat oven to 375°F. Place sheets of foil on countertop for cooling cookies.

7. Remove roll from freezer; remove wrapping. Cut roll into 3/8-inch-thick slices. Place slices 2 inches apart on ungreased baking sheet.

8. Bake one baking sheet at a time at 375°F for 7 to 9 minutes or until edges of cookies are very lightly browned. *Do not overbake.* Cool 2 minutes on baking sheet. Remove cookies to foil to cool completely.
Makes about 3 dozen cookies

POLVORONES (DUST BALLS)

1 Butter Flavor CRISCO® Stick or 1 cup Butter Flavor CRISCO® all-vegetable shortening
2 cups confectioners' sugar, divided
2 teaspoons vanilla
2 cups all-purpose flour
$1/2$ teaspoon baking soda
$1/8$ teaspoon salt
2 cups finely chopped hazelnuts (also called filberts)

1. Heat oven to 350°F.

2. Combine 1 cup shortening, 1 cup confectioners' sugar and vanilla in large bowl. Beat at medium speed with electric mixer until well blended.

3. Combine flour, baking soda and salt in medium bowl. Add to creamed mixture; mix well. Stir in hazelnuts and mix well.

4. Roll dough into walnut-size balls and place on ungreased cookie sheets about $1/2$ inches apart. Bake at 350°F for 15 minutes or until edges begin to brown lightly. Cool on cookie sheets until cool enough to handle, but still warm. While still warm, roll in remaining 1 cup confectioners' sugar; place on cooling racks to cool completely.

Makes about 4 dozen cookies

MANGO BREAD

2 cups all-purpose flour
$1^1/2$ cups granulated sugar
$1/2$ teaspoon salt
2 teaspoons baking soda
1 teaspoon baking powder
1 teaspoon ground cinnamon
$1/4$ teaspoon ground ginger
$3/4$ cup CRISCO® Canola Oil
3 eggs, beaten
1 teaspoon vanilla
2 cups fresh ripe mango, peeled and diced
$3/4$ cup golden raisins
$3/4$ cup macadamia nuts, chopped
$1/2$ cup grated coconut

1. Heat oven to 350°F. Spray two 9×5-inch loaf pans with CRISCO® No-Stick Cooking Spray. Dust with flour; set aside.

2. Combine flour, sugar, salt, baking soda, baking powder, cinnamon and ginger in large bowl.

3. Combine oil, eggs and vanilla in medium bowl; mix well. Add to flour mixture; mix well. Fold in mango, raisins, nuts and coconut.

4. Pour batter into prepared loaf pans. Bake at 350°F for 45 to 60 minutes or until wooden pick inserted into center of each loaf comes out clean and loaves are golden. Cool in pans 10 minutes. Turn out onto cooling rack; cool completely.

Makes 6 to 8 servings per loaf

PEANUT BUTTER PIZZA COOKIES

1¼ cups firmly packed light
    brown sugar
¾ cup JIF® Creamy Peanut
    Butter
½ CRISCO® Stick or ½ cup
    CRISCO® all-vegetable
    shortening
3 tablespoons milk
1 tablespoon vanilla
1 egg
1¾ cups all-purpose flour
¾ teaspoon salt
¾ teaspoon baking soda
8 ounces white baking
    chocolate, chopped
Decorative candies

1. Heat oven to 375°F. Place sheets of foil on countertop for cooling cookies.

2. Combine brown sugar, peanut butter, ½ cup shortening, milk and vanilla in large bowl. Beat at medium speed of electric mixer until well blended. Add egg. Beat just until blended.

3. Combine flour, salt and baking soda. Add to creamed mixture at low speed. Mix just until blended.

4. Divide dough in half. Form each half into a ball. Place 1 ball of dough onto center of ungreased pizza pan or baking sheet. Spread dough with fingers to form a 12-inch circle. Repeat with other ball of dough.

5. Bake one baking sheet at a time at 375°F for 10 to 12 minutes or until lightly browned. *Do not overbake.* Cool 2 minutes on baking sheet. Remove with large spatula to foil to cool completely.

6. Place white chocolate in a shallow microwave-safe bowl. Microwave at 100% (HIGH) for 30 seconds. Stir. Repeat at 30-second intervals until white chocolate is melted.

7. Spread melted white chocolate on center of cooled cookies to within ½ inch of edge. Decorate with candies. Let set completely. Cut into wedges. *Makes 2 pizzas*

Peanut Butter Pizza Cookie

PUMPKIN CAKE WITH ORANGE GLAZE

CAKE

        2 cups firmly packed light
            brown sugar
    ³/₄ Butter Flavor CRISCO® Stick
            or ³/₄ cup Butter Flavor
            CRISCO® all-vegetable
            shortening plus additional
            for greasing
        4 eggs
        1 can (16 ounces) solid-pack
            pumpkin (not pumpkin
            pie filling)
    ¹/₄ cup water
    2¹/₂ cups cake flour
        1 tablespoon plus 1 teaspoon
            baking powder
        1 tablespoon pumpkin pie
            spice
    1¹/₂ teaspoons baking soda
        1 teaspoon salt
    ¹/₂ cup chopped walnuts
    ¹/₂ cup raisins

GLAZE

        1 cup confectioners' sugar
    ³/₄ teaspoon grated orange
            peel
        1 tablespoon plus 1 teaspoon
            orange juice
        Additional chopped walnuts

1. Heat oven to 350°F. Grease 10-inch (12-cup) Bundt pan. Flour lightly.

2. For cake, combine brown sugar and ³/₄ cup shortening in large bowl. Beat at low speed with electric mixer until creamy. Add eggs, 1 at a time, beating well after each addition. Stir in pumpkin and water.

3. Combine cake flour, baking powder, pumpkin pie spice, baking soda and salt in medium bowl. Add to pumpkin mixture. Beat at low speed with electric mixer until blended. Beat 2 minutes at medium speed. Fold in ¹/₂ cup nuts and raisins. Spoon into prepared pan.

4. Bake at 350°F for 55 to 60 minutes or until wooden pick inserted in center comes out clean. Cool 10 minutes before removing from pan. Place cake, fluted side up, on serving plate. Cool completely.

5. For glaze, combine confectioners' sugar, orange peel and orange juice in small bowl. Stir with spoon to blend. Spoon over top of cake, letting excess glaze run down side. Sprinkle with additional nuts before glaze hardens.

Makes one 10-inch bundt cake (12 to 16 servings)

Pumpkin Cake with Orange Glaze

GLAZED CHOCOLATE POUND CAKE

CAKE
- 1¾ **Butter Flavor CRISCO® Stick or 1¾ cups Butter Flavor CRISCO® all-vegetable shortening plus additional for greasing**
- 3 **cups granulated sugar**
- 5 **eggs**
- 1 **teaspoon vanilla**
- 3¼ **cups all-purpose flour**
- ½ **cup unsweetened cocoa powder**
- 1 **teaspoon baking powder**
- ½ **teaspoon salt**
- 1⅓ **cups milk**
- 1 **cup miniature semisweet chocolate chips**

GLAZE
- 1 **cup miniature semisweet chocolate chips**
- ¼ **Butter Flavor CRISCO® Stick or ¼ cup Butter Flavor CRISCO® all-vegetable shortening**
- 1 **tablespoon light corn syrup**

1. For cake, heat oven to 325°F. Grease and flour 10-inch tube pan.

2. Combine 1¾ cups shortening, sugar, eggs and vanilla in large bowl. Beat at low speed with electric mixer until blended, scraping bowl constantly. Beat at high speed 6 minutes, scraping bowl occasionally. Combine flour, cocoa, baking powder and salt in medium bowl. Mix in dry ingredients alternately with milk, beating after each addition until batter is smooth. Stir in 1 cup chocolate chips. Spoon into prepared pan.

3. Bake at 325°F for 75 to 85 minutes or until wooden pick inserted in center comes out clean. Cool on cooling rack 20 minutes. Invert onto serving dish. Cool completely.

4. For glaze, combine 1 cup chocolate chips, ¼ cup shortening and corn syrup in top part of double boiler over hot, not boiling water. Stir until just melted and smooth. Cool slightly. (Or place mixture in microwave-safe bowl. Microwave at 50% (MEDIUM) for 1 minute and 15 seconds. Stir. Repeat at 15-second intervals, if necessary, until just melted and smooth. Cool slightly.) Spoon over cake. Let stand until glaze is firm.

Makes 1 (10-inch) tube cake

ROASTED ALMONDS

- 2 **tablespoons CRISCO® Canola Oil, divided**
- 1 **pound whole blanched almonds**
- 2 **teaspoons ground cinnamon**
  Confectioners' sugar

1. Heat 1 tablespoon oil in large skillet over medium heat until hot. Add ½ pound almonds. Cook and stir until evenly browned. Sprinkle with 1 teaspoon cinnamon; stir well. Place on paper towels to drain. Dust with confectioners' sugar to taste.

2. Repeat with remaining ingredients.   *Makes 1 pound nuts*

Crisco.com We cook.

CLASSIC CRISCO® DOUBLE CRUST

2 cups all-purpose flour
1 teaspoon salt
³/₄ CRISCO® Stick or ³/₄ cup
   CRISCO® all-vegetable
   shortening
5 tablespoons cold water (or
   more as needed)

1. Spoon flour into measuring cup and level. Combine flour and salt in medium bowl.

2. Cut in ³/₄ cup shortening using pastry blender or 2 knives until all flour is blended to form pea-size chunks.

3. Sprinkle with water, 1 tablespoon at a time. Toss lightly with fork until dough forms a ball. Divide dough in half.

4. Press dough between hands to form 5- to 6-inch "pancake." Flour rolling surface and rolling pin lightly. Roll both halves of dough into circle. Trim one circle of dough 1 inch larger than upside-down pie plate. Carefully remove trimmed dough. Set aside to reroll and use for pastry cutout garnish, if desired.

5. Fold dough into quarters. Unfold and press into pie plate. Trim edge even with plate. Add desired filling to unbaked crust. Moisten pastry edge with water. Lift top crust onto filled pie. Trim ¹/₂ inch beyond edge of pie plate. Fold top edge under bottom crust. Flute. Cut slits in top crust to allow steam to escape. Follow baking directions given for that recipe.

Makes 1 (9-inch) double crust

CLASSIC CRISCO® SINGLE CRUST

1¹/₃ cups all-purpose flour
¹/₂ teaspoon salt
¹/₂ CRISCO® Stick or ¹/₂ cup
   CRISCO® all-vegetable
   shortening
3 tablespoons cold water

1. Spoon flour into measuring cup and level. Combine flour and salt in medium bowl.

2. Cut in ¹/₂ cup shortening using pastry blender or 2 knives until all flour is blended to form pea-size chunks.

3. Sprinkle with water, 1 tablespoon at a time. Toss lightly with fork until dough forms a ball.

4. Press dough between hands to form 5- to 6-inch "pancake." Flour rolling surface and rolling pin lightly. Roll dough into circle. Trim circle 1 inch larger than upside-down pie plate. Carefully remove trimmed dough. Set aside to reroll and use for pastry cutout garnish, if desired.

5. Fold dough into quarters. Unfold and press into pie plate. Fold edge under. Flute.

6. For recipes using a baked pie crust, heat oven to 425°F. Prick bottom and side thoroughly with fork (50 times) to prevent shrinkage. Bake at 425°F for 10 to 15 minutes or until lightly browned.

7. For recipes using an unbaked pie crust, follow directions given for that recipe.

Makes 1 (9-inch) single crust

MA'MOUL
(DATE PASTRIES)

FILLING
- 1 pound chopped pitted dates
- 1/2 cup water
- 1/4 cup granulated sugar
- 1 teaspoon almond extract
- 2 tablespoons fresh grated orange peel
- 1/2 teaspoon ground cinnamon

PASTRY
- 1 Butter Flavor CRISCO® Stick or 1 cup Butter Flavor CRISCO® all-vegetable shortening
- 1/4 cup granulated sugar
- 3 tablespoons milk
- 1 tablespoon rosewater or water
- 2 cups all-purpose flour
  Confectioners' sugar

1. For filling, combine dates, water, 1/4 cup sugar and almond extract in small saucepan. Bring to a boil over medium-high heat. Reduce heat to low; simmer 4 to 5 minutes, stirring often, until mixture becomes a thick paste. Stir in orange peel and cinnamon. Remove from heat; cool.

2. Heat oven to 300°F.

3. For pastry, combine 1 cup shortening and 1/4 cup sugar in large bowl. Beat at medium speed with electric mixer until well blended. Beat in milk and rosewater. Beat in flour, 1/4 cup at a time, until well blended. Knead dough in bowl until dough holds together and is easy to shape.

4. Pinch off walnut-size piece of dough. Roll into ball. Pinch sides up to form pot shape. Fill center with level tablespoonful of date filling. Pinch dough closed; press to seal. Slightly flatten and smooth top. Place on ungreased baking sheets about 1 inch apart.

5. Bake at 300°F for 16 to 20 minutes or until firm and set. *Do not allow pastries to brown.* Cool on baking sheets 3 minutes; transfer to cooling rack. Sprinkle with confectioners' sugar while still warm. Cool completely.

Makes about 2 1/2 dozen pastries

Background. . . . . . .

These cookies are traditionally served in Syria during the Easter Holiday.

Ma'moul (Date Pastries)

Crisco.com **We cook.**

CHOCOLATE FUDGE PIE

1 unbaked Classic CRISCO®
  Single Crust (page 21)
1/4 CRISCO® Stick or 1/4 cup
  CRISCO® all-vegetable
  shortening
1 bar (4 ounces) sweet
  baking chocolate
1 can (14 ounces) sweetened
  condensed milk
1/2 cup all-purpose flour
2 eggs, beaten
1 teaspoon vanilla
1/4 teaspoon salt
1 cup flake coconut
1 cup chopped pecans
  Unsweetened whipped
  cream or ice cream

1. Heat oven to 350°F.

2. Melt 1/4 cup shortening and chocolate in heavy saucepan over low heat. Remove from heat. Stir in sweetened condensed milk, flour, eggs, vanilla and salt; mix well. Stir in coconut and nuts. Pour into unbaked pie crust.

3. Bake at 350°F for 40 minutes or until toothpick inserted in center comes out clean. Cool completely on cooling rack.

4. Serve with unsweetened whipped cream or ice cream, if desired. Refrigerate leftover pie.
  Makes 1 (9-inch) pie (8 servings)

PEACHY BLUEBERRY PIE

1 unbaked Classic CRISCO®
  Double Crust (page 21)
4 cups peeled and thinly
  sliced fresh ripe peaches
1 1/2 cups fresh blueberries,
  washed and well drained
1 cup plus 2 tablespoons
  granulated sugar, divided
2 tablespoons cornstarch
2 teaspoons vanilla
1/4 cup milk

1. Heat oven to 350°F. Combine peaches, blueberries, 1 cup sugar, cornstarch and vanilla in large bowl. Mix gently until cornstarch is dissolved and fruit is well coated. Pour into unbaked pie crust. Moisten pastry edge with water. Cover pie with top crust. Trim 1/2 inch beyond edge of pie plate. Fold top edge under bottom crust; flute. Cut slits in top of crust to allow steam to escape.

2. Bake at 350°F for about 35 minutes. Remove from oven; brush top with milk and sprinkle with 2 tablespoons sugar. Return to oven and continue to bake for an additional 15 to 20 minutes or until peach-blueberry mixture bubbles and crust is golden. Let rest 10 minutes before serving.
  Makes 1 (9-inch) pie (8 servings)

Chocolate Fudge Pie

SPICED CRANBERRY–APPLE SOUR CREAM COBBLER

4 cups cranberries, washed
6 Granny Smith apples, peeled and sliced thin
2 cups firmly packed light brown sugar
1 teaspoon ground cinnamon
1 teaspoon vanilla
¼ teaspoon ground cloves
2 cups plus 1 tablespoon all-purpose flour, divided
4 tablespoons butter, cut into pieces
2 teaspoons double acting baking powder
1 teaspoon salt
½ CRISCO® Stick or ½ cup CRISCO® all-vegetable shortening
1½ cups sour cream
2 teaspoons granulated sugar
Cinnamon or vanilla ice cream

1. Heat oven to 400°F. Combine cranberries, apples, brown sugar, cinnamon, vanilla, ground cloves and 1 tablespoon flour in 3-quart baking dish; mix evenly. Dot top with butter.

2. Stir together remaining 2 cups flour, baking powder and salt in medium bowl. Cut ½ cup shortening in using pastry blender or 2 knives until medium-size crumbs form. Add sour cream; blend well. (Dough will be sticky.) Drop dough by spoonfuls on top of fruit mixture. Sprinkle with granulated sugar. Bake at 400°F for 20 to 30 minutes, on middle rack, until top is golden. Serve with cinnamon or vanilla ice cream, if desired.   *Makes 6 to 8 servings*

Kitchen Hint. . . . . .

Lucky enough to have some leftover cobbler? Store it in the refrigerator for up to two days. Reheat it, covered, in a 350°F oven until warm.

Crisco.com **We cook.**

PEANUT BUTTER AND JELLY COOKIES

1 Butter Flavor CRISCO® Stick or 1 cup Butter Flavor CRISCO® all-vegetable shortening
1 cup JIF® Creamy Peanut Butter
1 teaspoon vanilla
²/₃ cup firmly packed light brown sugar
¹/₃ cup granulated sugar
2 eggs
2 cups all-purpose flour
1 cup SMUCKER'S® Strawberry Preserves or any flavor

1. Heat oven to 350°F.

2. Combine 1 cup shortening, peanut butter and vanilla in food processor fitted with metal blade. Process until well blended and smooth. Add sugars; process until incorporated completely. Add eggs, process just until blended. Add flour; pulse until dough begins to form ball. *Do not over process.*

3. Place dough in medium bowl. Shape ¹/₂ tablespoon dough into ball for each cookie. Place 1¹/₂ inches apart on ungreased cookie sheets. Press thumb into center of each ball to create deep well. Fill each well with about ¹/₂ teaspoon preserves.

4. Bake at 350°F for 10 minutes or until lightly browned and firm. Cool on cookie sheets 4 minutes; transfer to cooling racks. Leave on racks about 30 minutes or until completely cool.

Makes about 5 dozen cookies

CITRUS–GINGER COOKIES

1 Butter Flavor CRISCO® Stick or 1 cup Butter Flavor CRISCO® all-vegetable shortening
1¹/₂ cups granulated sugar
1 egg
2 tablespoons light corn syrup
1 teaspoon vanilla
3 cups all-purpose flour
1 tablespoon ground ginger
2 teaspoons baking soda
¹/₂ teaspoon fresh grated orange peel
¹/₂ teaspoon fresh grated lemon peel
¹/₂ teaspoon fresh grated lime peel

1. Combine 1 cup shortening and sugar in large bowl. Beat at medium speed with electric mixer until well blended. Beat in egg, corn syrup and vanilla until well blended.

2. Combine flour, ginger and baking soda in small bowl. Add to creamed mixture. Add orange, lemon and lime peel until well blended.

3. Shape dough into two rolls about 2 inches in diameter. Wrap tightly in plastic wrap; refrigerate 3 hours or overnight.

4. Heat oven to 350°F.

5. Slice dough about ¹/₈ inch thick. Place slices 2 inches apart on ungreased cookie sheets. Bake at 350°F for 6 to 8 minutes or until lightly brown. Cool on cookie sheets 4 minutes; transfer to cooling racks.

Makes about 7 dozen cookies

SFINCE DI SAN GIUSEPPE (ST. JOSEPH'S RICOTTA PUFFS)

FILLING
- 1 pound ricotta cheese, drained
- ½ cup confectioners' sugar
- 4 ounces grated dark chocolate
- ¼ cup candied fruit, finely chopped
- 1 teaspoon orange extract
- 1 teaspoon vanilla

PUFFS
- 1 cup water
- ½ Butter Flavor CRISCO® Stick or ½ cup Butter Flavor CRISCO® all-vegetable shortening
- 1 tablespoon granulated sugar
- ½ teaspoon salt
- 1 cup sifted all-purpose flour
- 4 eggs, beaten
- 1 teaspoon fresh grated lemon peel
- 1 teaspoon fresh grated orange peel
- Chocolate chips, melted (optional)

1. For filling, combine all filling ingredients in large bowl; mix well. Refrigerate while making puffs.

2. For puffs, heat oven to 450°F. Combine water, ½ cup shortening, granulated sugar and salt in medium saucepan. Bring to a boil over medium-high heat; stir well.

Add flour, stirring vigorously, until mixture leaves sides of pan. Remove from heat; let cool.

3. Slowly add eggs, beating vigorously, to cooled flour mixture. Add lemon and orange peel; mix well.

4. Spray baking sheets with CRISCO® No-Stick Cooking Spray. Drop tablespoonfuls of batter 2 inches apart onto baking sheets.

5. Bake at 450°F for 15 minutes. *Reduce oven temperature to 350°F.* Bake an additional 15 to 20 minutes or until golden. Cool completely on cooling rack.

6. To assemble, cut puffs in half horizontally. Spoon ricotta filling into bottom half. Cover with top half. Drizzle with melted chocolate, if desired.   *Makes about 18 puffs*

Background. . . . . .

This dessert is traditionally made on March 19, the feast day of St. Joseph. They appear in bakeries weeks before and are still there weeks after March 19. These delightful treats are delicious any time of the year.

Sfince Di San Giuseppe (St. Joseph's Ricotta Puffs)

Crisco.com **We cook.**

RASPBERRY AND CREAM PIE

CRUST
1 unbaked Classic CRISCO®
    Single Crust (page 21)

RASPBERRY LAYER
3/4 cup granulated sugar
1/4 cup cornstarch
1/8 teaspoon salt
1 3/4 cups water
1 package (3 ounces)
    raspberry flavor gelatin
1 package (12 ounces) frozen
    unsweetened raspberries

CREAM LAYER
1 package (3 ounces) cream
    cheese, softened
1/3 cup confectioners' sugar
1 teaspoon vanilla
1/8 teaspoon salt
1 cup whipping cream,
    whipped

SAUCE
2 squares (1 ounce each)
    unsweetened baking
    chocolate
1 tablespoon Butter Flavor
    CRISCO® Stick or
    1 tablespoon Butter
    Flavor CRISCO®
    all-vegetable shortening
3/4 cup confectioners' sugar
1/8 teaspoon salt
    About 2 tablespoons hot
    milk

1. For crust, prepare and bake 9-inch single crust as directed. Cool crust completely.

2. For raspberry layer, combine granulated sugar, cornstarch and 1/8 teaspoon salt in medium saucepan. Gradually stir in water. Cook and stir on medium heat until mixture comes to a boil and is thickened and clear. Add gelatin. Stir until dissolved. Stir in raspberries. Refrigerate until slightly thickened.

3. For cream layer, combine cream cheese, 1/3 cup confectioners' sugar, vanilla and 1/8 teaspoon salt in medium bowl. Beat at medium speed with electric mixer until smooth. Beat in whipped cream. Spread half of cream mixture on bottom of cooled baked pie crust. Top with half of raspberry mixture. Repeat layers. Refrigerate 1 hour.

4. For sauce, combine chocolate and 1 tablespoon shortening in small microwave-safe bowl. Microwave at 50% (MEDIUM) for 1 minute. Stir. Repeat until melted and smooth. (Or, melt on rangetop in small saucepan on very low heat.) Stir in 3/4 cup confectioners' sugar and 1/8 teaspoon salt until fine crumbs form. Stir in milk, a little at a time, until mixture is of desired consistency. Drizzle over raspberry layer and edge of crust. Refrigerate at least 1 to 2 hours before serving. Refrigerate leftovers.

Makes 1 (9-inch) pie (8 servings)